Warner Juvenile Books Edition
Copyright © 1988 by United Feature Syndicate, Inc.
All rights reserved.

Warner Books, Inc., 666 Fifth Avenue, New York, NY 10103
A Warner Communications Company

Printed in the United States of America
First Warner Juvenile Books Printing: September 1988
10 9 8 7 6 5 4 3 2 1

Library of Congress Cataloging in Publication Data

Gilchrist, Guy.
    [Steggie makes a friend]
    Guy Gilchrist's Steggie makes a friend: a Tiny Dinos story about shyness. – Warner Juvenile Books ed.
    p.   cm.
    Summary: A painfully shy dinosaur gets the courage to speak to another youngster after a misunderstanding and makes a new friend.
    [1. Dinosaurs – Fiction. 2. Bashfulness – Fiction. 3. Friendship – Fiction.] I. Title. II. Title: Steggie makes a friend.
PZ8.3.G39Gs 1988   87-35407
[E] – dc19
    ISBN 1-55782-100-3

FOR STEGGIE'S FRIEND, CAROLINE

Guy Gilchrist's Steggie Makes a Friend

A Tiny Dinos Story About Shyness

WARNER
JUVENILE
BOOKS

A Warner Communications Company
NEW YORK

Steggie was a stegosaurus who was utterly, shudderly shy.

He couldn't even say "Hi" back when someone else said "Hi."

He would have liked to say "Hi" back,
and make new friends and play....
But Steggie was utterly, shudderly shy
and "Hi" back he just could not say.

So, Steggie kept pretty much just to himself on the beach building castles of sand, till Playful Plateo came by one day with a sand shovel in his hand.

"Hi! Nice castle you've got there!" said Plateo in a loud and playful way. "I love to build sand castles, Stegg! Come on, let *me* play!"

"Plateo wants to play with *me*?!"
Steggie thought as his face turned red.
He tried to reply, but he was so shy...
he wound up saying nothing instead.

"Well! What do you know?!!" thought Plateo, "he must think he's too good for me!" Then he madly stomped Steggie's castle down...

and escaped on a vine from a tree!

Then Steggie got his courage up and roared "WHY DID YOU DO THIS TO ME?!!"

"'Cause you didn't want me to play with you!" sobbed Plateo, perched in the tree.

"I *DID* want you to play with me! *I DID!*" was Steggie's cry. "It's just that I have trouble expressing myself! I'm utterly, shudderly shy!"

Plateo sighed, "I know what you mean! Making new friends for me is a hassle! My problem's not shyness, it's bad-temper-highness... just look what I did to your castle!"

"Yeah!" grinned Steggie. "Look at this! You stomped it and you killed it! There's just one way to pay me back. And that's help me rebuild it!"

"*You bet I will!*" said Plateo. "We can build one to the sky! Let's build it fourteen miles long and sixteen miles high!"

So they built one,
though not quite that big...
still pretty tall and snappy!

And Steggie made a friend that day, and was utterly, shudderly happy.